DATE DUE

JAN 3 0 1986	
MAR 2 9 1986	
MAY 1 6 1986	
APR 1 7 1988	

AMERICAN MEDIA:
ADEQUATE OR NOT?

First in the fourth series of Rational Debate Seminars
sponsored by the American Enterprise Institute
held at
The Madison Hotel
Washington, D.C.

AMERICAN MEDIA: ADEQUATE OR NOT?

Philip L. Geyelin
Douglass Cater

RATIONAL DEBATE SEMINARS

American Enterprise Institute
for Public Policy Research
Washington, D.C.

2nd Printing, February 1972

Library of Congress Catalog Card Number 70-128373

FOREWORD

The American Enterprise Institute selected its topic for this debate by Mr. Geyelin and Mr. Cater before Vice President Agnew made his first speech about the media. We point this out for two reasons: the issue was already apparent before the Vice President spoke; the solutions should be the concern of the whole spectrum of American political thought.

Since the debate we have had indications that concerned groups are following up on some of the suggestions of the two principal speakers. This is particularly gratifying to the American Enterprise Institute, which seeks to stimulate thoughtful consideration of solutions to public policy problems.

July 14, 1970

William J. Baroody
President
American Enterprise Institute
for Public Policy Research

CONTENTS

FIRST LECTURE

PHILIP L. GEYELIN

> Yet the first bringer of unwel-
> come news
> Hath but a losing office, and his
> tongue
> Sounds ever after as a sullen bell,
> Remember'd knolling a departed
> friend.
>
> *(Shakespeare: Henry IV, Part II)*

Do the communications media present an adequate picture of American society to the public today? The short answer, not without considerable significance, is that there is no answer because nobody really knows. The executive branch appoints commissions to study crime, violence, foreign aid, the shipping industry, the military establishment. Congress studies almost everything, including itself, but only in the most peripheral way does either branch poke into the news business. No institution in our society, except perhaps the Church, enjoys such freedom from scrutiny and comprehensive analysis and no institution operating as a free enterprise has the same immunity from government investigation or control, leaving aside, of course, the licensing of television stations. Even in the case of FCC licensing of television outlets, however, the regulators are usually careful not to appear to be trampling on sacred rights —there is no Pure Food and Drug Act to control the quality of news reports. There are no standards for newspapers or television stations such as those governing everything from the safety of aircraft to the dimensions of a two-by-four, because the federal government, whether the executive branch or the Congress, is well aware of how quickly media representatives take the First, as it were, resisting the first hint of intrusion with a claim of constitutional immunity.

If the government, for its part, is nervous about transgressing the First Amendment's guarantees, the communications media themselves are just as cautious about creating any mechanism, from the British-style Press Council to an ombudsman of some sort, to police or even to study itself. The American Society of Newspaper Editors engages in some self-analysis, but little of it is either very penetrating or very self-critical and a lot of it is self-congratulatory. Journalism schools subject the news media to scholarly analysis. But the fact remains that we do not have a very sound basis for judging the performance of this vital business, industry-wide, in all its myriad aspects.

The inhibitions against governmental inquiry or formal self-inquiry into the news business are dangerous, in one sense, for the obvious reason that frailties and

foibles and failures which go undetected, or unac-
knowledged, are likely to go uncorrected. But there is
a greater off-setting danger to the integrity of a free
press from either government intimidation or government regulation—even formal self-regulation. So a
good argument can be made for the system as it is,
with responsibility largely vested in the individual newspaper or television station or network, and in the last
analysis, in the individual owner or publisher, or editor,
or the reporter who initiates the process of bringing the
news to the public. For in the best of these enterprises,
and among the best of these professionals, there is a
natural discipline at work—a continuing awareness of
the obligations as well as the benefits of the First
Amendment, and of what could happen if its special
license were ever to be restricted or revoked. Good
newsmen, if we can accept the assumption that there
are good newsmen in large numbers, probably agonize
more over their performance under this special constitutional grant of immunity than men in other industries under government regulation who, just because
they *are* controlled, have less compunction about devot-
ing time and energy in trying to fight free from their
fetters.

Beyond this there is a sort of built-in ombudsmanship in the communications field by the very nature of
the product and the relationship of the customer to it.
Newspaper and television stations are subject to a unique
form of consumer pressure because the total product

of a newspaper, or a television station for that matter, unlike anything else that is produced and marketed daily, is exposed to every customer, every day. A man may drive a Chevrolet and know little about what is under the hood—and still less about the quality of a General Motors truck. People buy insurance policies without any clear understanding of what they are getting or any guarantee that a subsequent claim will be paid. A housewife may sample some of the offerings of her favorite supermarket but she cannot get around to sampling them all; she cannot even be sure what ingredients went into her children's favorite soft drink. It might be said that you also cannot thoroughly measure the value of everything that goes into your daily newspaper or the evening broadcast. But you can at least see it or hear it—all there is of it, all there is going to be—and judge for yourself. And people do not hesitate to judge; on a daily basis all sorts of people—cab drivers and cabinet members, scholars and scientists, husbands and housewives—render their verdicts with relentless fidelity in letters and telephone calls.

Because the communications media are being monitored openly, regularly, and often mercilessly, the question before us today is being continuously answered by the news consumer every day in his own way. And that of course is what makes the question such a difficult one; consumer tastes in news and news analysis are highly personal, heavily colored, often deeply prejudiced, and very nearly impossible to categorize. There is no one judge; Vice President Agnew's standards, for instance, are not Senator Eugene McCarthy's standards, although both share a loathing of, to take a random example, the *Washington Post*. This is the first part of our problem—who is to judge? And by what standards and on what evidence in a country of more than 1,700 daily newspapers, 8,500 weekly newspapers, over 7,000 broadcasting stations, and any number of magazines of news or opinion?

The easy answer is that there is no judge who can rightly claim to know with any certainty whether the communications media present an adequate picture of American society to the public today, in large part because of the size and diversity of the media. But no end of people think they know, so we cannot leave it at that. One way to proceed might be to work our way back through the question, in an effort to break the big rock into more manageable little rocks.

1. What, for example, is "the public"? A considerable proportion of the estimated 62 million newspaper buyers in the United States spend a very large amount of time with the sports pages, or the comics, or the women's section, merely skimming the news which is now so readily available by osmosis from television. While it can be argued that more people would spend more time on the news pages if the news were better presented, the fact remains that the public, for our purposes, must be defined in terms of some smaller slice of the total reading or viewing audience: those of mod-

erate intelligence, with some degree of concern, a certain level of learning—and a reasonably long attention span. How big this group is, and whether it ought to be bigger—these are interesting questions, but they probably bear at least as much on the nature of our society or the quality of our educational system as they do on the performance of the communications media.

2. What do we mean by "a picture of society"? Surely we do not just mean news stories or film footage chronicling events, riots, student protest, a presidential State of the Union message, the passage of a piece of legislation, the dedication of a new school house, a train wreck, or a flood. What we are talking about here, presumably, is not only the quality of life but the interplay of the government and the people in an effort to improve it. It is in the chronicling of this process that the media play their indispensable role as a two-way channel of communication between the government and the governed. Entertainment and amusement are part of the media's business. But our concern here presumably is with what the media do to inform, illuminate, stimulate, educate.

3. We come next to the word "adequate" and just how you define that determines all the rest. If "adequate" means reasonably good, especially compared with how the media do in other countries, the answer probably is Yes. Obviously we do better than the closed, Communist societies of Russia or mainland China, and also better by a considerable margin, for

many more of our people than, say India, whose most respected paper, the *Times of India,* has a circulation of little more than 150,000. Comparisons with the advanced nations of Western Europe are a somewhat closer thing. Britain's television newscasting is comparable to ours, but although British newspapers reach national audiences in that compact country, the best of them reach the fewest people; year-old circulation figures show a circulation of 334,000 for the highly respected London *Times,* only 281,000 for the equally respected *Guardian,* and 1.4 million for the only other first-class daily, the *Telegraph.* Circulation grows rapidly as quality deteriorates—2 million for the *Daily Mail,* almost 4 million for the *Daily Express,* and over 6 million for the worst of the lot, the weekly *News of the World.* In France, the government controls the television network and the leading wire service and exerts a heavy influence on the press—although it can be argued that this is not as decisive as you might think, judging from the way President de Gaulle lost his popularity and his hold on the public even while using the government's influence blatantly to silence press and TV criticism of his regime. The media in West Germany, and on the other side of the globe in Japan, are probably comparable in many ways to ours but it still seems safe to say that nowhere in the world do the people get a better picture of the society they live in than we do—though there might be some question about how much comfort there is in that.

4. Finally, what do we mean by "the media"? It, or they, come in all shapes and sizes, from tiny weeklies, to the largest American daily, the *New York Daily News*, with a circulation of a little more than 2 million, a tabloid mentality, and a reputation for balance and thoroughness which is far below that of the prestigious *New York Times*, with somewhat less than 900,000 readers, or the *Washington Post* or the *Chicago Sun-Times*, with circulations around the half-million mark. No single American newspaper, good, bad, or indifferent, reaches more than a tiny fraction of the total newspaper audience. The only national newspaper, distributed beyond a relatively tiny circulation area, is the *Wall Street Journal*, with eight publishing facilities across the country and a circulation of just over 1 million. So how do you judge the press, by its best dailies, reaching only a relative handful of people, or by its far smaller and much inferior smaller papers scattered by the hundreds across the country, strictly limited in the amount of attention they give to public affairs or national issues, inadequately staffed, and in many cases struggling to survive?

Network television, of course, is somewhat easier to rate and measure because so much of the same material shows up on the same tubes in the 57.5 million U.S. homes with black and white television and the additional 17.4 million homes which have color sets, according to the latest available statistics. But the share of the estimated 6½ hours of total viewing time per home, per day, which is devoted to watching newscasts, public affairs documentaries, or other material offering some glimpse of American society, varies widely with events; in any case it can only be a small part of the whole.

Even if some means existed for measuring the quality of radio and television and the press individually, this would provide an overly compartmentalized picture because increasingly, as newspapers have adjusted to the competitive threat of electronic news, it has become less easy to view them separately; more and more these two must be examined as complementary halves of the whole process of conveying a picture of society.

Television has compelled the press to go beyond the breaking news to present more in-depth analyses and interpretative reporting; TV in turn has reacted with more of the same in the form of documentaries. So the media must be looked at in their totality and in the way television newscasts and press reports interact competitively upon each other and just about the time you think you have understood how this works, it becomes necessary to take into account the performance of what is perhaps the most pervasive news force in the land— the two wire services. The overwhelming majority of American newspapers cannot afford to have a network of foreign correspondents or more than a one-man Washington bureau, if that. Some 1,250 papers subscribe to the service of the Associated Press and most of those rely heavily on wire service dispatches for their national and international news coverage. The United

Press claims 1,200 newspaper clients (many newspapers subscribe to both services). The effect of this, of course, tends to give a greater degree of homogeneity to newspaper coverage of all but local news—although this still allows however for infinite variations in the way the news is played.

Much the same can be said of the broadcasting business; the Associated Press has over 3,000 broadcast stations as its clients, the United Press has about the same number; thus a very large part of the fare on an average newscast is shaped, if not dictated, by wire service stories. Needless to say these two big news agencies are hotly competitive and while UPI is number two, and tries harder, what this so often means in the news business is a bigger effort to dramatize the news, to needle a story, as the phrase goes, to sensationalize in a way calculated to catch the eye of an editor on deadline somewhere across the country. The vigor with which this competition is pressed puts a heavy premium on being first—not necessarily with the best story, not necessarily with the most comprehensive or the most balanced or thoughtful or deliberate story but the *first*. So when you talk about the media you are not talking about a simple instrument.

Having broken the question down, and perhaps demonstrated how essentially unanswerable it is in any absolute sense, perhaps it can now be reassembled in a somewhat different and more complicated form; do television and the press, together with the wire services, do as good a job as they could in presenting an accurate, balanced, comprehensive, unprejudiced picture of society—which is to say our problems and what we are doing or not doing about them—to that segment of the public which is interested enough, intelligent enough, and concerned enough to care?

Now the answer has to be No, and the interesting question becomes: Why not?

The answer is No, not only because the job is probably impossible, or because there can be nothing but the most arbitrary standards for judging what an accurate picture of society might be but because the errors and weakness and failures in the performance of the media are plainly there for all to see. We have mentioned the competitive pressures on the wire services, and the inevitable effect this has on depth and balance and all the rest. The point need not be labored that this applies as well across the board, wherever there is competition, which is almost everywhere, in some form and to some degree. Newspapers and television stations do not compete for favor in terms of their news coverage alone by any means. But news coverage is a big part of it and such is the advanced state of communications today, that newsmen must hustle all the harder to keep ahead. This is not merely a matter of a dollar-and-cents commercial interest in being first, or being more arresting, or more titillating, although you have only to look at the big circulation papers to conclude that sensation sells. It is also a matter of professional pride. So, one way or another there is a premium on speed and attention-getting, at the expense of all the other things that might make for a more accurate picture of society.

Other frailties of the media can be quickly noted, largely because they are human and to some extent inevitable.

People are more inclined to read or watch what interests them, and without trying to transfer the onus from the producer to the customer, it follows that the media are sorely tempted to give their audiences what they are thought to be most attracted to—excitement, novelty, calamity, all things aberrational. This assessment of what people want is not casually arrived at; men who are in business to make money tend to study the market rather carefully, and never mind whether the result is an adequate picture of society. So we hear a great deal more about the campuses where there is unrest than we do about the large majority of campuses where there is quiet. We hear about the problems that are currently, shall we say, fashionable, and we hear about them in such volume that inevitably the picture is distorted and we lose sight of the norm. Airplanes that crash are more interesting than those that don't; young people on heroin are more interesting than those who aren't; those who go to jail rather than be drafted are more interesting than those who don't. And because people will not read or watch things that don't interest them, we don't hear about the norm until we have become so sated by the abnormal that the norm becomes abnormal and therefore interesting.

Not much more needs to be said about the innate flaws; they have been there all along and they will doubtless remain to some degree for this is part of being a private enterprise peculiarly immune by constitutional degree from public regulation or investigation. They are as much a part of the media as the more mundane frailties that affect us all; incompetence, over-ambition, personal prejudice, sloth—except in the case of the news media there may be, if anything, a little less of them, and particularly there is probably less of the one thing most often attributed to newsmen—prejudice, a lack of objectivity—tilt. It is curious how often this word "objectivity" comes up, as if there were, or could be, a genuinely objective man. As David Brinkley and others have argued, better to judge the product than the man, better to apply a test of fairness, in what actually appears in print or on television screens, than objectivity in the person who brings it to you.

Even fairness, of course, is very much in the eye of the beholder. But it is at least a simpler test to apply—simpler, for example, than the easy accusation that most newspapermen and television commentators are "liberals." This is the charge that is in vogue at the moment—in 1948, Harry Truman could charge that a majority of newspapers, which favored Thomas E. Dewey for President, was anti-liberal. In any case, it is much too simple a charge particularly when it is put forth by Vice President Agnew in terms of some sort of Eastern seaboard, Establishment conspiracy. Undeniably a few of the most prestigious papers on the infamous Eastern seaboard are liberal, or perhaps more correctly, progressive, in their orientation. Undeniably, a case could be made that the average newsman in Washington is more likely to be comfortable with liberals or progressives or even moderates or whatever you wish to call them than with conservatives, which tends to mean more comfortable with Democrats than Republicans, although even those party lines are obviously far from clear.

In any case you have to ask yourself who is prejudiced in this matter and whether this itself may not be a distortion encouraged at this particular time in our political history for partisan political purpose. Because the thing about the average newspaper or television working stiff is that he moves freely, and to a far greater extent than most people, in *all* camps, those of the right, those of the left, those of the middle, those at the wildest extremes. He moves, he observes, he compares; and if he is more at home in one camp than another you have to wonder why men who are paid, and usually encouraged, to try to be impartial and factual and fair find the moderates, or the progressives, or the liberals, if you will, more compatible and more congenial. It is sometimes said that newsmen identify with the left and the poor and the disadvantaged, because they themselves are overworked and underpaid, and while there might be a germ of truth in this, as it applies to younger reporters especially, even they are less underpaid than they used to be. And it can hardly be said to apply to the stars of the television news shows. Whatever the case, there is once again a kind of built-in gyroscope to deal with this tilt, to the extent that it exists, because you cannot seriously argue that the working stiffs lean toward the left, without conceding in all logic that their bosses, the proprietors of newspapers and local television outlets, have an equally natural leaning towards the right, toward conservative thinking—the same natural leaning that many big and little businessmen have. With the possible exception of the Johnson-Goldwater campaign in 1964, it is quite safe to say that a very large majority of newspapers give editorial support and/or endorsement to the Republican candidate for President every time.

Too much, in short, can be made of the Agnew argument that the Eastern Establishment is in charge, and that its liberal instincts pervade the media; the media are far too diffuse and many-headed for that. Liberal bias, in short, does not go very far in explaining why the media do not do a better job than they do in presenting an accurate picture of American society to the public.

That said, it must be added that the Vice President's campaign against the press and the television networks cannot be lightly brushed aside; it has stirred more than enough public support to justify closer examination of what he is saying and why the public is responding. Obviously he has struck a nerve, and it is important to know why, and how he did it even while making what is on its face a bad case, indeed the wrong case, against the media.

Apart from simple invective and overheated rhetoric, Mr. Agnew talks about news monopoly, when he is not talking about news bias, and it is hard to see how he could have argued that case less effectively. In the first place, he went all the way from Washington to Montgomery, Alabama (which is one of the very few towns in America where all the media outlets are under a common ownership) and from this vantage point he singled out the Washington Post Company on grounds of monopoly. His point was that this company owns television stations, including one in Washington, as well as *Newsweek* magazine. It is a curious point, at best, since the *Post* is opposed by two other newspapers in Washington and both its television holdings and *Newsweek* of course have vigorous competition. Even so, the Vice President could have made a bad argument more interesting if he had bothered to study the matter at all; he could have noted that the *Post* and the *New York Times* are co-owners of the international edition of the *Herald Tribune;* that both operate flourishing news services which bring their product to several hundred newspapers across the country; that their influence, in fact, is wider than most people would suppose.

But even if Mr. Agnew had made the best case it would have been a poor one because it is nonsense to talk about the *Washington Post* or the *New York Times* and not mention, for example, the Scripps-Howard newspaper alliance, which includes 17 newspapers and five radio-TV interests; or the Gannett news service, which presides over four radio stations, two television stations, and 33 newspapers; or the Ridder Publications, with 11 newspapers, and extensive radio and television interests; or the Hearst newspapers, with nine papers and four radio-TV interests; or the 15 papers operated by Copley news; or the 22 newspaper members of the Newhouse chain which also includes seven television stations and 20 nationally distributed magazines. We have no way of knowing, of course, why the Vice President raised the question of monopoly; but the way he dealt with it suggests an answer. The *New York Times* supported Hubert Humphrey in 1968; the *Washington Post* plainly favored him; but the Scripps-Howard papers, for one example, endorsed the Nixon-Agnew ticket.

It might be noted, just in passing, that the Vice President did not mention another devout supporter of the Nixon-Agnew ticket and the Republican party, Mr. Walter Annenberg, who presumably received his reward, the post of ambassador to the Court of St. James. Before his recent sale of the *Philadelphia Inquirer*, Mr. Annenberg owned or had interests in the *Philadelphia Inquirer*, the *New York Morning Tele-*

graph, the *Daily Racing Form, Seventeen* magazine, *TV Guide,* and the *Philadelphia Daily News* (which is to say one of the two evening papers as well as the only morning paper in Philadelphia).

Given this kind of balance and fine impartiality on the part of the Vice President, it is no wonder that those in the media were quick to find the most blatant kind of political partisanship in his attack, and that some saw it strictly in terms of attempted intimidation. It is hard to see it otherwise; for the simple fact is that the monopoly argument won't wash. Few have made the case against it more persuasively than Mr. Raymond B. Nixon, a professor of journalism at the University of Minnesota, in testimony before the Senate Judiciary Subcommittee on Antitrust and Monopoly during hearings on March 19, 1968 on the so-called Failing Newspaper Act. Professor Nixon supported this proposed measure, which would relax certain provisions of the antitrust laws in order to enable newspapers to share joint facilities and services in the interests of economy and staying alive. And he did so for interesting reasons, chief among which were his contentions that newspapers today, even while declining in numbers, are under sharper competition than ever before because of the growing challenge from radio and television. Mr. Nixon also sees a decline in partisanship by the U.S. press. "Newspapers no longer are started or kept alive for purely political reasons as they were even down to the early part of this century," he told the subcommittee.

"The modern political party or pressure group has a public relations director and makes use of a wide variety of media. Neither does the average reader buy a daily for political reasons; he expects his newspaper to report the news and views of all major political groups. Even that traditional voice of U.S. Republicanism, the *New York Herald Tribune*, could not find anyone to save it once it started downward in circulation and advertising."

To be sure, Mr. Nixon did note that "only 45 of the 1,500 daily newspaper cities in the United States had two or more locally competing dailies at the beginning of 1968; thus 1,455 cities might be termed commercially noncompetitive as far as daily newspapers alone are concerned." He went on to say, however, that "when *all* daily media voices in the same 1,500 cities are included we find that there are 4,879 competing voices in 298 cities, and that only 202 single-voice cities remain." What is more, he said, examination of the hard core 202 single-voice cities reveals that at least 92 are suburban cities in densely populated metropolitan areas where the lack of local competition is "completely meaningless." When weekly newspapers are taken into account, he added, "there remain only 61 cities where a single daily appears to be without significant local competition for both news and advertising."

Mr. Nixon's concluding argument is worth quoting as a concise "state of the media" message on the monopoly question:

The extent to which radio and television compete with newspapers in bringing news and opinion to the public varies according to locality. Most broadcasting stations at least subscribe to a news service such as the Associated Press or United Press International and regularly broadcast news summaries. Even this much news serves as a "sword of Damocles" over the head of any newspaper publisher who might be tempted to withhold or distort news that he had received from the same service. In addition, the broadcasting of political events and speeches in many ways gives the public a better check on the accuracy of newspaper reporting than was possible in the preelectronic era of hotly competitive but violently partisan local papers.

When news magazines, suburban papers and other types of specialized print media are brought into the picture, along with radio and television, there can be no doubt that more American communities now have daily access to a far larger volume of information, opinion and entertainment than ever before. The principal media not only compete vigorously with each other: they also supplement and complement each other in a manner that was impossible when newspapers alone were the chief means of mass communication.

So much for monopoly, and so much for the merits of the Vice President's argument. It has none, or very few. And yet it did strike a nerve. Clearly, a great many people in this country, judging from the mail and the phone calls that followed the Vice President's attack on the media, were quick to rise up in anger against the press and television. While some of this sentiment was extreme and hate-filled—and a fact of life which does not tell much about the quality of the media—it is only fair to say that a lot of serious people admired what the Vice President was doing even while disagreeing with the way he was doing it. And at least one respected figure, ABC's television commentator, Howard K. Smith, declared in a recent interview in *TV Guide* entitled "There is a Network News Bias" that he agreed "we made the mistakes [the Vice President] says we made." That Mr. Smith is in a very small minority in his profession takes nothing away from his assertions that most news reporters are dogmatic liberals with "a strong leftward bias [and] a set of automatic reactions"; that they tend to "oversimplify" the news, "falsify the issues," and pay too much attention to negative news. Deep down, many of Smith's colleagues would agree with some of what he has said, and we have dealt with some of these weaknesses of the media already.

But Mr. Smith's mea culpa on behalf of the media has some of the quality of a self-inflicted wound, a hint of masochism, and perhaps even just a suggestion of the very weakness that Mr. Smith deplores—a very human yearning on the part of newsmen to say the shocking, unexpected thing. In any event, better and more balanced judgments of the performance of the media under pressure are available and one of the best of them is in a chapter of the Kerner Commission Report entitled "The News Media and the Disorders." After studying the record of the media in the 1967 summer rioting in the cities, the commission reached three conclusions:

First, that despite incidents of sensationalism, inaccuracies, and distortions, *newspapers, radio and television on the whole, made a real effort to give a balanced factual account of the 1967 disorders.*

Second, despite this effort, the portrayal of the violence that occurred last summer failed to reflect accurately its scale and character. The overall effect was, we believe, an exaggeration of both mood and event.

Third, and ultimately most important, we believe that the media have thus far failed to report adequately on the causes and consequences of civil disorders and the underlying problems of race relations.

The commission went on to expand on these three points and its verdict is worth quoting at some length because rarely is the performance of the press and television examined by so distinguished a group of citizens with such care under what might be called a crisis situation:

Despite the overall statistical picture, there were instances of gross flaws in presenting news of the 1967 riots. Some newspapers printed "scare" headlines unsupported by the mild stories which followed. All media reported rumors that had no basis in fact. Some newsmen staged "riot" events for the cameras. . . .

Reporters uncritically accepted, and editors uncritically published, the inflated figures leaving an indelible impression of damage up to more than ten times greater than actually occurred. . . .

. . . we believe that it would be imprudent and even dangerous to downplay coverage in the hope that censored reporting of inflammatory incidents somehow will diminish violence. . . . But to be complete, the coverage must be representative. We suggest that the main failure of the media last summer was that the totality of its coverage was not as representative as it should have been to be accurate. . . .

. . . Many of the inaccuracies of fact, tone and mood were due to the failure of reporters and editors to ask enough tough questions about official reports and to apply the most rigorous standards possible in evaluating and presenting the news. . . .

The news media have failed to analyze and report adequately on racial problems in the U.S. and, as a related matter, to meet the Negro's legitimate expectations in journalism . . . news organizations failed to communicate to both their black and white audiences a sense of the problems America faces and the sources of potential solutions. . . .

We cannot envision a system of governmental restraints . . . failings of the media must be corrected and the improvement must come from within the media. . . .

The Commission's major concern with the news media is not in riot reporting as such, but in the failure to report adequately on race relations and ghetto problems and to bring more Negroes into journalism.

It is difficult to argue with most of this, not only as a critique of the riot coverage in 1967 but as a critique of the media day in and day out, in its continuing effort to render some kind of coherent picture of American society to the public. A final caveat is in order, however, about all of this because what has been said so far still does not entirely explain the phenomenon of the Vice President's success in rousing a large segment of the American public against the media. What a lot of people are really saying, when they say that they want a better balance or less bias or a different picture of society than the one they are getting, is that they don't like the one that they are getting; that they don't want to hear bad news; that they want a picture of society more congenial to what they think it is or wish it was. This is the audience the Vice President is playing to, and it is not just the bigoted American, or the vindictive American, but the Complacent American, the comfortable affluent American, undisposed to be interrupted and therefore quick to conclude, when there is word of trouble—of a war gone wrong, of an environment gone sour, of a society gone haywire—that the media are overdoing it for commercial gain. It would be nonsense to argue that the media does not overdo it, or that this isn't the consequence of competitive pressure, or even that a certain hysteria or at least professional fadism does not afflict the industry. We saw that in the wild way CBS played the Democratic Convention in 1968, the incendiary juxtaposition of the most hairy riot film with shots of reaction on the convention floor. But at least part of the problem is that communications themselves have reached such an advanced state that an extremely subtle and sophisticated use of the phrase "benign neglect" by Daniel P. Moynihan in a confidential memo to the President of the United States can become mildly distorted even in its first printing in the *New York Times* and grossly distorted as it races across the country on wire service teletypes. In the end, it was all too often twisted into a recommendation for neglect, in a benign way, not of the more inflammatory aspects of the race debate but of the blacks themselves. It is too easy now to smother the country, to shock a whole populace simultaneously, to burst into 50 million living rooms with bad tidings. And so who could argue that this does not call, as the Kerner Commission and others have suggested, for an extra measure of restraint.

But one has to be careful, nonetheless, what one is restraining. It is all very well not to want to hear bad news, but if the press is not prepared to go out and look for it, who else will tell us that the Vietnam war has become unwindable; that we are doing unremediable damage to our air and water; that a senator or even an associate justice of the Supreme Court has a conflict of interest; that racial tension is on the rise. It is an odd thing, when you think about it, for the Kerner Commission, on the one hand, to urge the media to dig more deeply into the underlying causes of violence, and then when the media does just that, for the silent majority to deplore its emphasis on bad news. And it is a healthy and encouraging thing when the *Wall Street Journal* can report, as is did on March 13, 1970, that the Washington press corps is coming under "growing pressure, especially from liberals." A capsule item in that paper's weekly "Washington Wire" goes on to say:

Democrats charge that reporters are intimidated by the Nixon regime, fail to ask hard questions about Vietnam, Mideast, urban racial policies. It's a major Muskie theme. Other Democrats seek newsmen's favor by attacking Administration demands for their films and notes. . . . Civil rights groups fighting the Carswell nomination charge the press is deserting their cause by saying Nixon's Court choice can't be beaten. A Civil Rights Commission spokesman accuses newsmen of neglecting racial problems, diverting public attention by building up the environmental issue.

Nixon advisers complain the press is conjuring up a recession. Mine Workers chief Boyle wins some headlines by charging he gets unfair news treatment.

And again, in a column by Henry Brandon in the March 14 issue of the *Saturday Review:*

Significantly, several old left Democrats in Congress have recently complained to me about the mass media in terms similar to the Vice President's. They too blame television for the near state of anarchy in this country; they are convinced that the overexposure of radical students and Black Panthers and the overemphasis on demonstrations and riots have done them in and account for their own political distress. They feel that much of the public blames the Democratic Party for having tolerated these excesses and for having indulged in political permissiveness. These voters are turning, therefore, to the Republican Party in the hope that it will prove to be tougher and more effective in restoring law and order. A situation is thus developing where television and the press are being blamed by both Republicans and Democrats for the troubled state of this nation. . . .

So it is a nonpartisan affair, this sudden turning against the media. And while nobody would deny that the media could do a better job, and present a better balanced picture of American society to the public, there is something rather comforting about the evenhandedness with which the media is now being attacked from all sides. "Yet the first bringer of unwelcome news hath but a losing office, and his tongue sounds ever after as a sullen bell. . . ."

SECOND LECTURE

DOUGLASS CATER

It was, I have been assured, sheer accident that our topic today bears close resemblance to a theme being regularly sounded by the Vice President of the United States. Let me preface my remarks by stating flatly that any similarity between his criticisms and mine are purely coincidental. The last person whom I would wish to have elevated to the role of arbiter for the communications media in this country would be one holding the official position of Spiro T. Agnew.

Nevertheless, I was stimulated by Mr. Agnew's remarks to review my own appraisal and critique of our communication system written 12 years ago. I was both impressed and depressed by the experience. Impressed that what I wrote then still struck me as relevant and true. Depressed that so little has happened in the intervening period to elevate the dialogue on the role and responsibilities of the mass media. The entire Agnew assault and the media response begin to remind me of two professional wrestlers who seem to get pleasure out of their grunts and groans. The debate on communications appears, like Little Orphan Annie, never to grow an inch.

The Vice President essentially made two points: one, that the media fail to communicate the picture of reality that accords with the picture he holds. Two, that the picture communicated by the media is controlled by a small mysterious group known as "they." Mr. Agnew didn't get very specific about who "they" are. But "they" are to blame for our communication failures.

Now the interesting thing about Agnew's analysis is that Stokely Carmichael and Jerry Rubin and other leaders of the radical left would agree with both points. So would George Wallace. The devil theory of the mass media rallies a diverse band of brothers.

But more disturbing to serious critics is that Agnew has stirred a response among a much wider public than the extremists on the right and the left. He has apparently touched a sensitive nerve. We need to study this phenomenon. It is not enough to respond in the fashion of the bumper sticker I read recently in Los Angeles: "Will the silent majority please shut up."

"Do the communications media present an adequate picture of American society to the American public today?" One media critic, who is widely quoted but little read and even less understood, suggests that this is not a proper question. The question ought to be turned around according to Marshall McLuhan. He argues that the media are not reflecting but shaping society. In an interview carried in *Playboy*, which is the clearest explication of his theories that I have come across, McLuhan states:

> All media, from the phonetic alphabet to the
> computer, are extensions of man that cause deep
> and lasting changes in him and transform his en-
> vironment. . . . But most people, from truck driv-
> ers to literary Brahmins, are still blissfully unaware
> of what the media do to them; unaware that be-
> cause of their pervasive effects on man, it is the
> medium itself that is the message, *not* the content,
> and unaware that the medium is also the *massage*—
> that, all puns aside, it literally works over and
> saturates and molds and transforms every sense
> ratio. The content or message of any particular
> medium has about as much importance as the
> stenciling on the casing of an atomic bomb.

McLuhan is a controversial and frequently confusing
critic. I am not certain that he himself fully under-
stands the full implications of his various insights. But
he was not the first to contemplate the shaping role of
the media. E. B. White, that sensitive observer of
mankind, wrote a short essay in the *New Yorker* back
in 1938 after he had witnessed a demonstration of
television. He concluded, "I believe television is going
to be the test of the modern world, and that in this new
opportunity to see beyond the range of our vision we
shall discover either a new and unbearable disturbance
of the general peace or a saving radiance in the sky. We
shall stand or fall by television—of that I am quite
sure." White went on to explain:

Television will enormously enlarge the eye's range, and, like radio, will advertise the Elsewhere. Together with the tabs, the mags, and the movies, it will insist that we forget the primary and the near in favor of the secondary and the remote. More hours in every twenty-four will be spent digesting ideas, sounds, images—distant and concocted. In sufficient accumulation, radio sounds and television sounds may become more familiar to us than their originals. A door closing, heard over the air; a face contorted, seen in a panel of light— these will emerge as the real and the true; and when we bang the door of our own cell or look into another's face the impression will be of mere artifice.

But E. B. White, too, was not the first to be concerned about this strange relation between image and reality. We must go all the way back to Plato. In the *Republic,* Plato relates the parable of the underground den in which human beings have been chained since childhood, positioned so that they can see only the shadows projected from behind against the den's inner wall. Plato concludes, "And if they were able to talk with one another, would they not suppose that they were naming what was actually before them?"

This interplay of image and reality fascinated me as a reporter in Washington long after I had forgotten Plato and before I had heard of McLuhan. For I observed that the image of government, projected by the media, was being accepted as the reality not only by the public but by those involved in government. I wrote in my book, *The Fourth Branch of Government*, that the news of government

has been known to assume a generative spirit of its own—in turn recreating the people and policies being publicized even as the Hollywood starlet is remade to fit the public stereotype. The reporter in Washington has witnessed on numerous occasions the phenomenon described by the psychologist when the mask of the man takes possession of the true self. More than witness, he has helped to shape the mask which transforms the public figure.

After four and a half years inside the White House, I can only say "amen" to this analysis. Communication media have a vast power to shape government—its policies and its leaders. This is not a strictly editorial power. It is the power to select—out of the tens of thousands of words spoken in Washington each day and the tens of dozens of events—which words and events are projected on the den's wall for mankind to see. Equally powerful is the media's capacity to ignore. Those words and events which fail to get projected on the den's wall might as well not have occurred.

My first criticism of the media is that they don't take themselves and their role seriously enough. You have only to read the minutes of the annual meetings of their professional associations to prove this point. A number of my colleagues in the press were offended by

the title of my book assigning the communicators to a
fourth branch of government. They felt contaminated
by the phrase. They refuse to admit that those who are
involved in the communications of a democracy play
a major role in its governance.

I do not profess to be an expert on the whole of
American society. But I strongly suspect that the role
of the communications media is pervasive throughout
its daily life. The media project the shadows by which
American society judges itself—whether we are pretty
or ugly, healthy or sick. In the age of television, we are
all more aware that each of us lives in a cubbyhole of
direct experience. We all spend more and more of our
lives, in E. B. White's phrase, viewing the secondary
and the remote, digesting ideas, sounds, images—distant
and concocted. How can any one of us judge whether
the images we see are an adequate picture of American
society today?

We are more image-conscious than our forefathers.
Marshall McLuhan argues that we need to be conscious
not only of images, but how the images are made and
their impact on us. He says:

In the past, the effects of media were experienced
more gradually, allowing the individual and society
to absorb and cushion their impact to some degree.
Today, in the electronic age of instantaneous communication, I believe that our survival, and at the
very least our comfort and happiness, is predicated
on understanding the nature of our new environ-

ment, because unlike previous environmental changes, the electric media constitute a total and near-instantaneous transformation of culture, values, and attitudes. This upheaval generates great pain and identity loss which can be ameliorated only through a conscious awareness of its dynamics.

These are abstract words but they may help explain some of the hostility toward the media which has been displayed by the silent and the not-so-silent majority. We don't know for sure what the media are doing to us but we are damned uncomfortable about it.

It is my assigned task to speculate on whether the picture of American society presented by the media is "adequate." At the risk of being charged with bias, I would like to register some doubts and to present two examples of faulty communication for which the media at least partly share the blame.

As the decade of the 1950s came to a close, the dominant image of America held by most Americans was of a quiet society afflicted with faint fears of being stagnant. Our great concern was to achieve a higher economic growth rate. J. K. Galbraith, a pace setter among idea men, had in 1958 published his book *The Affluent Society*. He devoted only a limited amount of attention to the poverty in our midst and pretty well confined even that, as Michael Harrington later pointed out, to "insular" rather than "endemic" poverty. John F. Kennedy found a convincing campaign theme in pledging to get America moving again. But when he

talked of millions of people going to bed hungry at
night, even close supporters thought he was laying it
on a bit thick.

The reality of that period was quite different. The
American economy may have been stagnant but American society was in tremendous ferment. During that
decade alone, there was a migration of over 8 million
Americans into the metropolitan areas. Since the start
of World War II, nearly two and a quarter million
blacks left the South and crowded into the northern
cities. Urban America was feeling the tremendous strain
on its facilities—schools, hospitals and clinics, welfare.
There was a rapidly growing crisis in the finance and
governance of the cities. Prosperous Americans were
fleeing to the suburbs.

And that crisis was not being adequately communicated. I was a reporter during that decade but, to
refresh my memory, I dispatched a researcher to the
Library of Congress to review the public record. My
conclusion is that the media did not serve as an early
warning system for the crisis that is being so widely
reported today. Poverty, as Harrington wrote in 1962,
was "invisible." It was not being heard, not being
communicated.

When President Johnson launched the war on poverty
in 1964, it was not in response to a great outcry from
the press and public. In fact, the situation was just the
reverse. One scholar, Elinor Graham, has observed in
an essay, "The Politics of Poverty":

The power of the Presidency to stimulate the news media into undertaking a massive effort to increase public awareness, if not to generate actual demands for government action, was dramatically demonstrated. This achievement should not, however, obscure the fact that demands for action directly focused upon poverty did not exist prior to the time that the Administration began to produce its new policy line.

An interesting sidelight is that in the early planning stages of the poverty war, the President's economic advisers were concerned primarily by the stagnation of the general economy *not* by the fast growing crisis of urban poverty. All this may suggest a failure of politics and economics. But, this afternoon, we are discussing the shortcomings of our communication system.

Let us turn to my second example. As the decade of the 1960s drew to a close, there were some rather startling statistical changes in America. The economy had achieved an unparalleled period of rapid growth. The increase in gross national product during the first eight years of that decade, measured in constant dollars, was greater than the entire GNP of 1938. To put it succinctly, in less than a decade, a second economy had been built as large as the national economy prior to World War II. At the same time, there was unprecedented spending by federal, state, and local governments on poverty-related programs. More families were moving out of poverty and at a faster rate than at any time in our nation's history.

Yet, if we looked, at the shadows on the wall of the den, we saw unmitigated misery. There was widespread public concern that we had become a sick society. Spokesmen, from George Wallace on the right to the extremists of the left and a good many in between, found agreement in the slogan "We never had it so bad." The picture we were seeing of ourselves led to growing despondency among many citizens over whether our society, as presently organized, can cure its ills.

I suggest that this, too, represents a failure of communication. It is, paradoxically, an opposite failure from my first example. During the late fifties, our communication media failed to serve as an adequate early warning system for troubles already on the horizon. During the late sixties, the media failed to discriminate adequately among the troubles in our midst. Like a stuck burglar alarm in a department store, the jangling of the media threaten to stimulate either public panic or public apathy or both.

These are blanket and highly subjective indictments, I realize. They are apt to provoke impatient reactions from reporters and editors alike. So why blame the media for all the sins of society? What about the experts in and out of the universities? What about politicians who claim to represent the people? Haven't they contribtued to the faulty picture of American society? The answer is that they certainly have. But our topic this afternoon is the media.

A more serious objection is that the mere statement of these inadequacies puts impossible demands on our communications media. Am I, to use Walter Lippmann's phrase, asking the reporter to serve as "the umpire in the unscored baseball game?" Nearly a half century ago, in his classic book *Public Opinion,* Walter Lippmann raised the question whether "news"—the product of the media—could ever be made to serve as the vehicle for communicating the "truth" about government or society. He reached a pessimistic conclusion. "If we assume . . . that news and truth are two words for the same thing, we shall, I believe, arrive nowhere," he wrote. The function of news, Lippmann pointed out, is "to signalize an event" whereas the function of truth is "to bring to light the hidden facts, to set them into relation with each other, and make a picture of reality on which men can act." Lippmann thus dismissed the communications media as the means to present an adequate picture of American society to the public. Instead, he advocated the creation of new institutions of "organized intelligence" which would serve as the purveyors of truth.

Looking at the situation nearly 50 years later, I am inclined to doubt that the roles of news and truth can be that neatly divided. I do not believe the leaders of the communications media wish to abdicate the task of bringing to light the hidden facts, setting them into relation with each other, and making a picture of reality on which men can act. That is the kind of journalism which wins awards in the industry.

There have been some noteworthy new organizations of intelligence since Lippmann wrote his book. The Council of Economic Advisers, the Bureau of Labor Statistics, and the Bureau of the Census supply vital and impartial statistics which have vastly improved the reporting on the nation's economy. Economic communications are no longer like umpiring an unscored baseball game. Similarly, a private institution such as Congressional Quarterly has provided better yardsticks for measuring and communicating an adequate picture of the legislative branch. Numerous enterprises—the Southern Regional Council, the Urban Institute, the Fair Campaign Practices Committee, etc.—have sprung up to provide the organized intelligence on complicated problems of American society. They have helped to create a more adequate picture. Many of them have been subsidized by foundations. I sometimes wonder what would be the condition of our communications if the media were not aided by this particular form of philanthropy.

But I do not believe it is the job of government or philanthropy to take over completely the organizing of intelligence. Our communications media are not paupers. They can afford to do a larger share of the digging and the fitting together and the reporting in depth. I learned in my journalist days that the really important reporting is expensive in time and money. It is easier and much cheaper to play follow-the-leader journalism—to read the clip files, think up a gimmicky new lead and practice armchair reporting. I watched a great deal of that kind while I was in the White House.

I marvel at the maldistrubution of reportorial resources. Hundreds of reporters are dispatched to cover the inquest at Chappaquiddick. Less than a half dozen give any systematic coverage to the education crisis in America which affects the lives of millions of children. Education appears to stand only slightly higher than religion as a journalistic beat.

To organize intelligence and present a more adequate picture of American society is going to require initiative from those involved with communications. It is time for them to be more than at best grudging, at worst hostile recipients of other people's ideas about taking up new responsibilities in a new era. I will be impressed when I see leaders from the press and television media, individually or in association, approach the universities and research institutes on better ways to organize intelligence about our society. We know, for example, that economic indicators have only limited value in revealing the social condition. Why aren't the media leading the effort to develop a set of social indicators that will provide reporters with meaningful yardsticks?

We live in an era when all our traditional institutions are under attack. The Establishment is suspect. Old and private arrangements can no longer be easily defended. The credibility gap looms before all who exercise power in our society, not simply the politicians.

Universities, foundations, churches—no institution has been exempt from searching reexamination by those who challenge the way our society works.

There is no reason why the institutions of the communications media should be exempt. They are crucially affected with the public interest. This does not call for government regulation in the manner of the public utilities. Far from it. But it does mean that there is a right of public review of how well the media are fulfilling their role.

Several ways occur to me for helping close the credibility gap and perhaps even improve media performance.

First, it is time for more public accounting of the problems of news management. How the news is managed has been kept in dark mystery even as the media strive to throw the fierce light of publicity on decision making elsewhere. It would be refreshing, first of all, for the public to know that the collecting, processing, and distributing of news require judgments all along the line. Human judgments. It would be even more helpful to credibility if there were more frank discussions and mutual criticism of human error in the managing of news. For too long the communicators have operated according to Randolph Churchill's dictum that "Dog don't eat dog." When someone commits folly, everyone else looks the other way. I think the *Washington Post* has started a healthy habit with its FYI editorials pointing out some of the problems of the press.

This needs to be carried further. No one can expect

self-criticism to be too rigorous. But there is no reason why the newspapers can't be sharply critical of television and television of the print media. And there is good reason to encourage more young men to follow the footsteps of A. J. Liebling and Ben Bagdikian as thoughtful critics of the media. Where are their successors?

Conceivably, the managers of the media would profit by including a wider group in their discussions of sensitive issues. Take television's handling of dissent in our society, for example. What are the firm and enduring guidelines? Obviously, television, like the other media, must be sensitive to early warnings of social discontent which could grow serious. There is long tradition supporting Jefferson's tolerance for "error of opinion so long as reason is felt free to combat it."

Has time and technology changed Jefferson's principle? He wrote in an age when the dissenter's views reached only the range of his voice or the tiny circulation of the pamphlet press. If dissent made sense, it would be picked up and echoed by others. But how does network television apply that limitation? Does TV's coast-to-coast range give the dissenter publicity advantages which the voice of reason is unable to combat? This is surely one of the most weighty issues of our age. But the public has little evidence of how seriously the networks are weighing it. Network practice appears to vacillate one way or the other as the winds of opinion blow.

Talk to television reporters themselves and they express bafflement about the management of the nightly news roundups. What are the standards for allocating the precious seconds? Who provides the editorial review to make certain that bias and sensation don't dominate the news. Print media leave a record that everyone can examine. But television writes news in the air.

A second area of public accounting goes to the economics of communications. We need the equivalent of a Royal Commission to inquire why there are so many exit routes from the media and so few entrances. Must we sit and watch while one great national magazine after another dies, usually from a surfeit of circulation? Is there something in the tax law that allows chain owners to bid for newspapers with different kinds of dollars than individual publishers? How can we provide new incentives to maintain diversity in the ownership of the media?

Must the public sit by mutely while the networks decide how many more minutes of advertising per hour can be crammed into TV programming? Is there a way for the public interest to be more adequately represented as cable TV and pay TV become part of the American way of life?

All these questions and others are worthy of legitimate public inquiry. The problem is how to set up proper institutions for such public inquiry. I doubt that a congressional hearing is an adequate forum and, considering the Agnew outburst, I would be suspicious of a presidential commission. Surely it ought to be possible for a leading school of communications, such as Columbia's, to take the initiative, with foundation backing, to establish a group of wise men, including communicators, dedicated to this mission.

A Commission to Investigate the Adequacy of Communications would not have a humble assignment. It might start from the bottom up by examining exactly what is the picture that reaches the public. Then it could proceed to define areas of organized intelligence that are missing in that picture. And, finally, it would come to the question of what role the media might be expected to play—the existing media and possibly newly created media.

I don't believe we should jump to the conclusion that our existing media represent the last word in communications. There is room for innovation. Yardstick media such as public television should be given a fair and well financed opportunity to prove their worth. Just as "Sesame Street" has demonstrated marvelous new techniques of stimulating preschoolers, there may be untried ways of reaching adults with a more adequate picture of the world beyond their immediate horizons.

It was my privilege to ride herd for the President on the legislation that created the Public Broadcasting Corporation. I believe it to be one of the more helpful initiatives in the communications field during the past few decades. But I am full of fears for public television. Hand-to-mouth appropriations as a means of financing it could lead to all sorts of hidden pressures that would destroy its integrity. I hope the statesmen of television will continue to give the corporation their strong support as they did when it was first launched.

In making this suggestion for a commission, I am well aware of the derisive greeting it will receive from many veterans in the communications field. I remember the abuse heaped on the Hutchins Commission, nearly a quarter century ago, even though it had been suggested and largely subsidized by Henry Luce. Reread this many years later, the Hutchins Report does not seem like such a radical document. Its main message was that the press could best maintain its freedom by becoming more accountable. Its most daring proposal was to create an agency, independent of government and of the press, to appraise and report annually upon the press.

The commission listed society's five expectations of the communications media:

1. A truthful, comprehensive and intelligent account of the day's events in a context which gives them meaning;

2. A forum for the exchange of comment and criticism;

3. The projection of a representative picture of the constituent groups in the society;

4. The presentation and clarification of the goals and values of the society;

5. Full access to the day's intelligence.

These are hardly a very startling set of expectations. It would be helpful if a new commission took a look to see whether we have moved closer or farther away from realizing them.

But the fact is that the communications business is often treated by its spokesmen as the last preserve of rugged individualism. Even as media have grown into vast corporate enterprises, its spokesmen keep up the pretense. The First Amendment is treated as an iron-clad bar against probing into the adequacy of communications, even as the publishers push for an act of Congress exempting them from certain provisions of the Antitrust Act.

Let me be clear. When I argue that the communications media are affected with the public interest, I am not talking about the official government's interest. They do not belong within Spiro Agnew's mandate. On the other hand, the concern for communications should not be limited to the communicators either. Other publics and other institutions have an important role to play in defining the problems and setting the goals. Other subsidies may be needed to stimulate innovators even as tax and license subsidies have helped those presently engaged in the business.

For we are discussing today the most critical function that holds a free society together—how it communicates. And the challenge in a society grown as big and vulnerable as ours is formidable. There is a story, perhaps apocryphal, that the dinosaur did not go out of existence because he was too big or too clumsy. What really happened was that he suffered a failure of communication. His brain did not transmit signals to his foot—and the foot back to the brain—rapidly and accurately enough to create a picture of reality on which the dinosaur could act. That story holds a lesson we should keep in mind.

REBUTTALS

PHILIP L. GEYELIN

It seems to me that what has happened here is that Mr. Cater and I have approached the question from opposite directions and come out at the same place, more or less.

Still, it would not do to accept all his criticisms of the media or even most of them. These are blanket and highly subjective indictments, I realize, and I wouldn't argue with that.

They are apt to provoke impatient reactions from reporters and editors alike, he goes on, and I wouldn't argue with that. I will try not to be impatient.

But I think one thing has to be emphasized because it seems to me it gets so easily lost when nonpractitioners inveigh against the news business in the main: and I'm not talking about magazines, and I'm not talking about special kinds of limited forms, I'm talking about the whole mass media, and it is a daily business, even hourly, even minute-by-minute, for the wire services or for a newspaper or for a newscaster on deadline. We may need a law to slow down the whole process, to make it mandatory for everybody to stop and think, let's say, for 24 hours before writing. Except that it simply wouldn't work.

I invite your attention to one striking example, the Supreme Court, which I covered sometime ago. As you know, there are little desks in front of the Court and tubes that go down and grown men crouch in a kind of airless, windowless cubicle underneath the bench and the decisions come down in a little capsule and they have to fire off, as fast as they can think and render—and you read a Supreme Court decision, as you know, from the back towards the front—a coherent account of what has happened.

I did it for the Dow Jones news ticker and there are a lot of people who are prepared to bet dollars and cents on the outcome of these decisions. They didn't want to wait 24 hours or 24 minutes.

They were waiting for word, for example, of the decision, which took a few years off my life, on the seizure of the steel companies by President Truman. On that particular day I scored a clean beat because the UPI tube jammed and the AP got the vote wrong. So it is on that kind of thing that you score these triumphs and it is a nutty arrangement.

But I've talked to Supreme Court justices urging them to lock us up in a room, if they will—one with windows, they can draw the shutters, if they're worried about signals—but let us study and reflect for, say, two hours before sending this really quite crucial information out. But they won't do it.

I don't know whether it has something to do with tradition or what it is but they won't do it. The fact of the matter is, the main reason they won't do it is because people want to know. This pressure is something people who haven't worked in the media don't understand.

Mr. Cater talks of organized intelligence centers and the role of the foundations in enriching the product with facts and figures but that is not what it's all about. Leaving aside whether people care what Ford or Brookings or the RAND Corporation thinks, actually they want to know what the government, which has the power and makes the decisions, thinks.

Leaving even that aside, the fact remains we are dealing in split seconds with what must be one of the world's most perishable commodities, today's news. You have to keep this in mind when you talk about reform, this competitive pressure, this crushing influence of the clock.

Mr. Cater, because he hasn't lived in it, doesn't take it much into account. Perhaps, because I have lived in it all of the time I've been in the business, I take it too much into account. Similarly, because he has worked on the other side, in government, he also sees the media in different terms than I do.

He concedes in passing that politicians and experts in and out of the universities contribute to the complications of the media and to the sins of society. They certainly have, he says, but our topic this afternoon is the media.

That's great. He seems to be saying that because we are talking about the media today we will visit the sins of society on the media today but I don't think it's that simple.

On the other hand, Mr. Cater also tends to see the communications media as something that is orchestrated by government or that it ought to be, something to be used and exploited, which, of course, it is, too often. But the media don't write the music; they record it.

I revert to my original point. A lot of people who don't like the music are blaming it on the record player. The fact remains that much of what is wrong about the picture the media presents is wrong because it was given out or revealed wrong.

I refer you to Phil Goulding's book which is just out, *Confirm Or Deny*. In instance after instance Phil records situations where he misled the public because he in fact was misled. There are at least five instances having to do with the capture of the Pueblo, with the attack on the Liberty, with the Air Force flight over the Pierrelatte nuclear installations in France, and so on.

I refer you to the current inability on the part of even the highest-level policymakers of the government to agree on what happened in March 1968 in the change in our Vietnam policy, and I ask you to tell me how the press could be expected then, or even now, to get it right, when Clark Clifford, the President of the United

States, Phil Goulding, and Tim Hoopes apparently can't straighten it out among themselves.

Or I ask you to consider the example of the 1950s, which Mr. Cater raises where it wasn't so much a question of government secrecy as just apparently of the press being asleep during a period of great social change.

Mr. Cater would have the press operate as an **early** warning system on the problems of the cities in the fifties. Ask yourselves what would have happened if the press had done so at a time when a war on poverty was clearly not uppermost among the priorities of the Eisenhower Administration or really on anybody's mind. The government controls the only really authentic banks of facts with which we have to deal. There are increasingly the foundations that Mr. Cater talks about. But the facts that we pay the most attention to necessarily are the facts that the government is paying the most attention to because those are the facts on which the government is going to make the decisions. And out of these banks of facts, the only ones which citizens have so far come to rely upon, the government would have extracted—indeed, did extract—material reinforcing the picture of an affluent society.

Had the press acted as an early warning system, had it said this was wrong, had it said, "We can see the beginnings of trouble," it would have been accused, as it is now, of alarmist, sensation-seeking reporting.

It seems to me that the press has an obligation to get into these things but essentially, if no leaders, if no politicians, if no congressman, if the President doesn't care and if the public doesn't care, it's a bit much to ask the press to care.

This is really what's happening now that the media are tackling environment with what some people consider is an excessive burst of energy and effort, afraid that this is bound to flag in time, that interest will flag even while the problem grows steadily worse. Now that the press is, in my judgment, acting very efficiently as an early warning system in this whole area of pollution and environment, the people are saying, "For God's sake, stop talking about it."

So it's not easy to strike the right balance. But I'm not sure an instrument as volatile as the daily press or TV is suited for early warning. Better a book, a Rachel Carson or a Harrington, who, incidentally, concedes the poverty issue was invisible in the fifties, or a Nader. Better a broader canvas and a longer lead time for that kind of role.

The point is that while there is an honored place for crusading reporting of the kind that appeals to academicians in remote places who are thinking ahead on problems that haven't really yet surfaced, news reporting is still essentially a daily business.

There is no point in giving it a primary role it doesn't have and then taking it to task for not fulfilling it.

It is time maybe to pay tribute. Mr. Cater has, I think, some very interesting ideas for reform. I'm still a little puzzled by this business about organizing intelligence about our society. For the press to get into the intelligence-organizing business, I would say, inevitably is for the press to compromise the process, to compromise the intelligence it itself organizes.

The Reader's Digest used to do this planting and digging and I think that's a mistake for us to do. I think we ought to be independent, as much as possible, of the organized centers of intelligence.

But he's dead right about some of the bad habits, the dogs don't eat dogs syndrome that he talks of, the really crucial lack of self-criticism. I don't find that hard to concede having conceived of the FYI editorials, which he graciously nods to in the *Washington Post*.

However, there is, incidentally, a reason with which I am thoroughly familiar. He says he can see no reason why newspapers don't take on television on the basis that they don't take on each other. I think I can testify that it's not all that easy. While we really do not harken, the way Mr. Agnew says we harken, this business of joint ownership of two kinds of media has its inhibitions.

I'd be interested in some kind of a royal commission to study the economics of the media. In fact, this is rather related to joint ownership of newspapers and television, because the latter provide generally steady and more than adequate profits for the capital with which to make it possible to publish better newspapers.

But I am worried about that word "incentives," whether they're tax incentives or whatever kind. The

French, for one example, have a variation on that and it turns out to be a very convenient handle on the media that I wouldn't want our government to have.

So I go back in the last analysis to the fundamentals. It was all very well to talk about organizing centers of intelligence and looking for new supplementary institutions feeding something more into the mix. But I do think that Walter Lippmann is a very poor witness. Mr. Cater quotes a 50-year-old book, by Mr. Lippmann, concluding, in one part that he dismisses the communications media as a means to present an adequate picture of American society; instead he, Mr. Lippmann, advocated the creation of new institutions.

Now, I don't doubt that he did 50 years ago but in the meantime, in fact, he subsequently created a new institution and he called it, for lack of a better name, Walter Lippmann. For eight years or so he ran the editorial page of the *New York World* before launching his own column, which made him an international intellectual force of really unparalleled influence.

That, in fact, is what he did in pursuit of truth as news and he used as his vehicle, I think it's worth noting, not some new organized institution, but the established, traditional communications media.

This encourages me. I'm encouraged to believe even that the current excesses of the media will correct themselves, not always in time, not always perfectly, but inevitably. And not because of new institutions or of government intervention or some formal structured devices set up by the media themselves for self-regulation—because I think they'll always shy away from that —but because of the customer.

Somehow that dinosaur image at the end doesn't quite fit for me. It is not that society is not getting signals rapidly enough or even accurately enough. It is getting signals too rapidly and too many of them. The circuit is overloaded and there's a real danger, I think, of overheating. People, I do think, on the other hand, have a way of showing when they've had too much, when they are sated. That's a part of the emotion I think the Vice President may be tapping in his own way, and this is no more than a sign to me that the sins of the media carry with them in the nature of things and in the nature of their relation with the consumer their own corrective, which, in our society, is likely to be the most healthy and reliable corrective we can apply. Thank you.

DOUGLASS CATER

I knew that Mr. Geyelin would hit me with the low blow that I have not worked for a daily paper. He forgets that I was the Washington correspondent for the Winston-Salem papers for a period of time. I met a deadline. I can't be dismissed that easily.

He makes another debating point. In his paper, he happened to pick my own home town of Montgomery, Alabama. He chastises Mr. Agnew for going there. He says Montgomery is one of the very few towns in America where all the media outlets are under a common ownership.

I didn't trust my own knowledge. I phoned a leading lawyer in Montgomery this morning. Montgomery has common ownership of its morning and afternoon papers but it has three separate television stations, none of which are owned by the newspapers. So that's for that.

As you no doubt perceive, we have tended to meet toward the middle. I find myself feeling many agreements with Mr. Geyelin because I think his criticism is more pervasive than he admits, whereas mine perhaps is less than I admit.

I agree wholeheartedly with his statement at the

beginning of his paper that no institution, "except perhaps the Church," has been so free from scrutiny as the media. Of late, the Church has been under considerable scrutiny so I wouldn't make even that exception.

He also says that the media are extremely cautious about creating mechanisms for studying themselves, and I would say "Amen" to that. One has only to read the minutes of the various professional associations of both the newspapers and the broadcast media to realize how much they shy away from anything that has a chance of becoming an institution for self-criticism.

I only partially agree with Mr. Geyelin's argument that there is a natural discipline at work among the best members of the press creating an awareness of obligations as well as responsibilities.

I do agree that among our best reporters, particularly here in Washington, there is a keen and continuing sense of responsibility. The system would break down if it were not for that.

I'm not sure how far you can extend this principle as a governing rule; nor do I think that it gets to some of my fundamental concerns about the role of the media in society.

Mr. Geyelin points to a built-in ombudsmanship but, when I talk to people, what bothers them most in dealing with media is how does one say something that really gets heard inside the silent vastness of one of the big media? I'm not aware of anything inside the TV media that is even equivalent to the letters to the editor column.

I think Mr. Geyelin makes good points when he compares our system with other systems in other societies. In 1958, I spent a year traveling around the world and looking at four separate communications systems: in England, Germany, India, and the Soviet Union. I came back more aware than ever that ours was unique. The media perform a function in our society which is different from any other system that I know of. To try to make comparison with the closed communication system of the Soviet society is totally fruitless.

Mr. Geyelin agrees that the question should be: Are the media as good as they could be? His own arguments point to fundamental problems that I had not considered in my paper. He says that at least part of the problem is that communications themselves have reached such an advanced state that an extremely subtle and sophisticated use of the phrase "benign neglect" by Moynihan in a confidential memo "can become mildly distorted even in its first printing and grossly distorted as it races across the country." Mr. Geyelin comments, "It is easy now to smother the country, to shock the whole populace simultaneously, to burst into 50 million livingrooms with bad tidings."

This is, I think, what causes us the trouble. The technology of the media has advanced so miraculously. Perhaps the time has come when we need to stand apart and try to figure out what the guys in the engine room are capable of doing under such a system.

I found more documentation than criticism in Mr. Geyelin's description of the men at the end of the tube in the Supreme Court. Obviously, this is a scandalous way to cover the Supreme Court. Even if the Supreme Court hasn't got enough communications sense to understand this, some independent group in our society should look at it and point it out for the scandal that it is.

I'm not interested, as certainly Mr. Geyelin is not interested, in developing a devil theory of communication. I don't think the shortcomings can be attributed to malicious wrongdoing by individuals or groups.

I was interested in Mr. Geyelin's description of the tilt of journalism in which he suggests that perhaps the liberalism of the reporter is counterbalanced by the conservatism of the editor and publisher. Maybe there would be a nice Ph.D. thesis for someone—to see exactly how that balance mechanism works out.

But I am more interested in his use of Raymond Nixon's analysis that there really are only 61 cities in America without significant local competition in the media. Competition is healthy, yes, but Mr. Geyelin points out that competition can often be the root cause of some of the distortions in communications.

I feel hopeful about the beginnings of media council in various communities. I was in Honolulu in January when the editors of the two leading papers, the heads of the TV stations, members of the university, and the general public spent a whole day discussing the creation of a media council in Honolulu. I believe it will come about. I hope that this proves to be a spreading practice.

I'm not as sanguine as Mr. Geyelin about the fact that the attack on the media is bipartisan. There is something to what people involved in policymaking are saying, no matter how badly they may say it. They are deeply concerned, as all of us are, about what it is that holds the society together, what it is that gives us the capacity to govern.

And although it is not the responsibility of the politicians to set the standards for a communication medium, nevertheless, it's somebody's job. It is somebody's job to look at how accurately the media shape the picture of society.

If you are composing music for a piccolo, you have to think of shrill tunes. Sometimes I have the feeling that the politicians, more than they themselves realize, find their tunes circumscribed by the sound range of the media.

I close by saying the same thing I said at the beginning. On one thing I am in total agreement with Mr. Geyelin. This job is not Mr. Agnew's. Thank you.

DISCUSSION

EDWIN TRIBBLE, Sunday Editor, *Washington Star*: I notice that both of our speakers mentioned self-criticism on the part of the media and I think that's something that we would all agree with. I would be curious to know their ideas on how that might be run off. Would this be done by people who are working for the media, in news or advertising, within the media, or would it be done in an independent magazine, or in a separate thing? What could you envision as a vehicle for this self-criticism?

MR. GEYELIN: Of course, there is one magazine, there is the Columbia *Journalism Review*, and I guess there are other magazines about the press, *Editor and Publisher*, and so forth.

But I would begin, I think, by somehow encouraging the members of the media to talk about each other. We report every industry, every institution. We report the government. We report the Church. We report everything except that, with the single exception really of the press section of *Newsweek* and *Time*, we don't report about each other. We don't talk about each other.

The *Wall Street Journal* does. I mean, the *Wall Street Journal* is prepared to do a very long front page study of the economic position of Time-Life. But by and large, we shy away from it. We don't even write about ourselves.

For example, if your paper or mine were to build a new building tomorrow, you'd merely have a very antiseptic story back on—at least we would—

(Laughter.)

—back in the back sections. We're very self-conscious about that.

I think the beginning of it is when we start treating the media for what they are, for what Mr. Cater called them in his book, *The Fourth Branch*. That's important. This is the fourth branch and we don't even discuss it in our own newspapers. I think we're really going in the tank for each other.

MR. CATER: I do think that there has been a very useful role played in the past when men decided to devoted their careers to becoming skillful and not just blunderbust critics of the media. I mention A. J. Liebling and Ben Bagdikian. Liebling is dead and Bagdikian is now in management.

A VOICE: News management. (Laughter.)

MR. CATER: We need new men to come along. I also think there should be ways of reporting and criticizing on TV the way a news story developed, particularly one that caused confusion and conflict.

I have often said to students that I wish the average

citizen could read his paper or watch his news show with the same sophistication that a journalist has. When we read a story, we put our minds to work in calculating what were the influences affecting that story. This kind of sophistication should be developed among the citizenry. Too often I find that if they think about the media at all, they think about them in such stark and simple terms that it's almost hopeless to develop a serious discussion.

CLARK MOLLENHOFF, Special Assistant to the President, The White House: I was a newspaperman once myself. (Laughter.) And I want to address myself to the period prior to the time I joined the White House staff.

I was writing Sigma Delta Chi reports as a Washington correspondent almost every year, for the period of the last 12 years. One thing that struck me in this business was the lack of knowledge of the newspaper business in the newspaper business. I'm talking in terms of the free press and fair trial issue and the fine knowledge that's needed in this area to really come to grips with the real problem. There are few people in the news business who are qualified to come to grips with it. Now I wrote reports after reports and I know Ted Koop (Columbia Broadcasting System) did. I know this is an area where Doug Cater has a great deal of depth knowledge. I know there are some others around here who do.

But, broadly across the newspaper business there is

not that kind of an understanding of such things as
shield laws. I don't know how many people in this room
know what a shield law is. When you put up your
hand be ready, now, to stand up and explain it in detail.

How many know the shield law well enough to really
explain it? (Two hands up.) That's a good indication.
The shield laws are the laws that have been suggested
from time to time and passed in a dozen states to protect
the reporter in his confidential sources. I'm not going
to call on you because you put your hand up and I
know you know all about it.

This is something that has come into the news and
into editorials recently in connection with the administration and the subpoenaing of reporters and records
and things of this nature.

In dealing with this it is necessary to have a clear
understanding of the shield laws and which confidential
sources you can refuse to disclose and which you can't.

I see many people who write loosely about this lawyer-
client relationship, the husband-wife relationship, and
the doctor-patient relationship. Most people in this
room probably do not know that there are great limita-
tions and restrictions on those confidential relation-
ships—that the lawyer-client relationship doesn't apply
to everything in their relationship with these people.

It applies to one little area where there has to be a
communication between the lawyer and the client to
take care of the client's interest and that's it. The fact
that some fellow is engaged in a robbery and runs up

to the lawyer's office and he's suffering from some wound or other, the lawyer cannot get into the position where he doesn't testify about the wound or anything like this. The only thing he can testify to is that a man came to his office in a certain stage, he was in this kind of condition. The confidential relationship covers only what the client said to the lawyer.

Now, with regard to the newspaper people generally. The only time there's a confidential relationship is when the information that came to the reporter is understood to be under a confidential relationship. Even then, there isn't any federal law to protect it.

We have some states where there are laws, and Sigma Delta Chi has very carefully stayed away from endorsing those shield laws because, you get into the position of trying to determine what is a professional journalist and what is not. There are some labor publications and some gambling sheets that might make the claim. It's a fine line. And what would you do, if you had these shield laws generally?

You could have a gambling sheet that might claim confidential sources. Writers for gambling sheets might use that as a shield for almost any crime.

In our own business we should know what the lines are in these areas. We should not be against cooperating in producing records, in giving testimony where crime is involved, unless we have an arrangement with a source and said clearly, "I'm going to protect you."

Then we have no legal right. It is only a professional

obligation. Then we should just go to jail. If there is a genuine confidential relationship, the newsman should go to jail. He should be willing to make the sacrifice. I don't know of too many who are doing that lately. I do know of an awful lot of uninformed news people who simply say I won't tell anything because I'm a newspaper reporter. They do not know what these rights and obligations are in this area.

Now let me say one other little thing. I'm not so concerned about the understanding by the publishers and the editors and all that other upper structure. I am concerned about reporters. I think that much of this problem would be solved if the reporters in this country—whether for radio or television—would decide themselves that every story they're going to write would be one they would like to use for research material two years later, five years later, or ten years later.

You'd be amazed how much more responsible that would make newsmen. You'd be amazed how many people dash off whatever takes care of the situation for the day.

The *New York Times* vs. *Sullivan* case is a great case from the standpoint of leading responsibility out the window. I think it went too far. There are too many people now who say, "Oh, hell, he's a public official." The *New York Times* vs. *Sullivan* case indicated we can say anything we want to about him, as long as they can't prove direct malice, and that's it.

I think that's gone too far. I think that there are

some circumstances where it has been beneficial. But all of this has led to an irresponsibility in certain areas, and I could go into the details but I won't. Thank you.

MR. GEYELIN: I can't pick up everything you said, Clark, but there is one thing about this willingness either to go to jail or tell the government, give the government your confidential notes.

This gets more complicated if you're talking as the government has talked about getting prints of the pictures you don't print, for example. That's one thing that the Justice Department or the FBI has asked the *Washington Post* to do and it isn't quite as simple, I think, as you put it.

A negative of a picture which we run in the paper, for example, which may not show any faces, when blown up may be able to be used to identify people who have taken part in a demonstration.

Now this is all very helpful to the police but it is not very helpful——

MR. MOLLENHOFF: (Interposing) But——

MR. GEYELIN: Let me just finish.

MR. MOLLENHOFF: Yes.

MR. GEYELIN: It is not very helpful——

MR. MOLLENHOFF: I really want to answer that.

MR. GEYELIN: But it is not very helpful to a newspaper.

We've just had a case out in Chicago recently, of the Chicago Bureau of *Newsweek*, in which confidential notes were turned over to a court or to the authorities with the identification of the source taken off and the notes all clipped and censored and edited so that there was nothing in them that would identify the source.

Even with that, I was told by the Bureau members of *Newsweek*, when I was out in Chicago the other day, that their sources in the area that they were working, which is not organized crime, it's the Black Panthers, and the students and so forth, have dried up.

Newsweek is considered out there to be in bed with the government, working for the government, a part of the law-enforcement process, and people who would talk to *Newsweek* before will not talk to them now.

In the case of photographs, it's even more complicated, because we had to send photographers out into the streets, on 14th Street in April 1968, to take pictures. They were in just about as much physical danger as we'd like to have them in the best of times. They're in very much more physical danger if they are taking pictures in an atmosphere in which it is known that pictures that don't even appear in the paper will be turned over to the authorities and that their notebooks will be turned over.

It makes it extremely hard in my judgment with that kind of a rule to do our business. A man has to be ready to go to jail. I was asked about this in a meeting of the staff of the *Post* the other day and I must say I don't know the answer to that. About the best that I could suggest was that we were in favor of improving conditions in jails. (Laughter.)

I don't know. It's a difficult thing to have a clearcut editorial policy on because it is a little more complicated.

MR. MOLLENHOFF: Let me explain one thing. I think the law enforcement agencies should use great restraint in this area of calling a reporter as a witness. If you can obtain the information from some other source, you should go to the other source. If you can obtain the information from other records, you should go to those other records.

However, there are a good many circumstances where reporters are present and where there is nothing confidential about what is taking place.

With regard to these photographs and so forth: Those photographs were taken for the purpose of being used on the air or in the newspapers in some respect or another; you just didn't happen to use them. Now, I don't think, under those circumstances, that the law enforcement body or the government should get into the question of whether you should or shouldn't have used those pictures in the paper. That's your editorial judgment and you should have the right to do what you want in that respect.

But there's another question. Should you, if you have material evidence to a crime and where there is no other way of getting the evidence, should you make it available? I know, as an investigative reporter over a long period, that you have on the staffs of your paper—and the *Wall Street Journal* and others—reporters who have worked with law enforcement agencies on investigative matters and you have tried to get action.

There is no rationale at all that can bar us from our role as a citizen in going forward and producing whatever evidence we have. I do think that there should be restraints on the part of the attorney general and on the part of U.S. attorneys so they do not come to you unless it's the last resort.

Let me take another little point or two. CBS had some interesting experience financing an invasion of Haiti. In this instance there was a group of revolutionaries who were going down to Haiti. Apparently they did not have much money and so they got an exclusive contract from CBS to film this.

Now getting that exclusive contract provided them with what they needed in the way of money to finance an invasion.

This gets to be a very fine line as to whether you're financing an invasion or whether you are engaged in enterprising reporting. We're all for enterprising reporting, but how enterprising should it be?

Now, to make a determination of this, the House Commerce Committee has been conducting an investigation. They have asked for and obtained the film that was taken. They got into the books of CBS to find out who authorized what payments to the revolutionaries. This happens to be a federal law violation and the investigations of it are not all over yet, although some have been prosecuted.

These are things that we should keep in mind as we resist. I think the newspapers should resist under circumstances where they can say: "You could get that same information from some other source. Don't be harassing our reporters and their sources." Perhaps there is reason for not cooperating if the newsman can say: "These law violations, whether they're in the gambling field, the liquor field or whatever field they might be, are things that would be accessible to you, if you were doing your job as a law enforcement officer."

But there are exceptions to this. Where those exceptions apply I think everyone in the newspaper business, like every citizen, should try to cooperate.

JACK E. BUTTRAM, Office of Senator Paul J. Fannin: You both agree the Vice President should not be the one who criticizes the media, seeking to reserve the right for meaningful criticism to internal, inside people. I don't quite follow the rationale that would limit the Vice President in his constitutional rights. I don't think you would allow the same type of rule to apply to, say, the U.S. Senate. Mr. Cater, would you deny Hubert Humphrey his constitutional right as a citizen?

MR. CATER: No. And I was being perhaps flippant. Obviously, the Vice President or Hubert Humphrey have got a right to say anything they want about the media. I hope they are not the meaningful critics of the media. I say that we need to create institutions of criticism. I believe that you can go a long way if you develop a sense of self-criticism within the communications media. But it's also a question of opening up the legitimate area of public oversight. I think it is rather curious that in an era where "the right to know" has been sounded rather relentlessly, the press or the media have regarded themselves as closed corporations. I think it is rather amusing when we suddenly read about *Newsweek* having this female problem on its hands. They never thought when they were writing a cover story about the rights of females that suddenly their own researchers were going to read it and apply its lessons at the office.

MR. GEYELIN: I would like to add one point. I didn't mean to make the argument that the Vice President didn't have the right. My point is that he did it so badly, he made such a bad case of such an interesting question that you had to wonder why he brought it up at all. The only explanation for making such a bad argument is not that he was suggesting a serious remedy, but that he was using or waving, the authority of the government. This does have some influence, particularly with respect to the Des Moines speech that had to do with the television stations, and indeed the Montgomery speech which had to do with newspapers owning television stations, because these newspapers at the time may have license applications. I think when the case is made that badly it does raise the issue of what is he trying to tell us and I think a lot of people—not us, I don't think, as much as others—came to the conclusion that what he was trying to tell us was you'd better cool it, you had better stop the commentaries after the President's press conferences.

MR. BUTTRAM: I confess a certain amount of frustration not in the news management, but in an inability to cope with what I consider unfair treatment from the press. If you recall, last year, at the beginning of the Nixon Administration, there were three or four stories on the front page of the *Post* about the alleged complicity of Strom Thurmond and David Packard in the awarding of certain textile contracts down South. I think Dave Broder was writing most of those stories. At the time, having had some expertise in the textile industry and some acquaintance with the problem, I talked to Dave and I said I had some information which bore on this. I said I thought it would provide something of the other side of the story. He said fine, send it to me and I'll write it. He did. Now, the other three stories had appeared on page one. The story he wrote appeared on page 11. How does the press secretary cope with this situation?

MR. GEYELIN: This is about the time that I identify myself as an editorial page editor. (Laughter.) You got robbed. Frankly I wouldn't argue with that. But I would also go back to what I said—that hour by hour, minute by minute we are exercising human judgment, and I don't think that there was a conspiracy to restrain the senator's point of view. I suspect that the story got sort of run down. It's always difficult to get the "catch up" story on the same page as the first story. The editor that made that decision may not have been the editor that made the first. One of the stories may have broken on a hot news day and the other may have come along on a slow news day.

MR. BUTTRAM: I don't say that it's a conspiracy myself. But as a person who deals with reporters, going to Clark's point, I find it not difficult to deal with reporters, because if I don't get good treatment this time I don't deal with them next time. It's the guy that writes the headlines, the make-up guy. This is the area of criticism. As a disseminator of news I find the greatest difficulty is in dealing with these unseen men in the news apparatus; I think this problem is one which perhaps the media themselves are not aware of. Somewhere in the media there must be a correcting influence. What we have had recently has been a kind of reaction, a gut reaction sometimes——

MR. CATER: Any group that works in the same physical area and rubs shoulders too long develops a habit of congeniality. This is true of doctors, lawyers, and everybody else. But when you look at the Washington press corps, there is enough influx, enough turnover. Compared to other professions, there's very little seniority system. A raw reporter can come in and, if he runs away with an important story, make the elders in the profession look pretty bad.

PROFESSOR HOWARD PENNIMAN, Georgetown University: Try a different point of view from what people have tried before. When I was interested in the 1967 elections in Vietnam, I watched several newspapers' coverage of them. If one studied the *Washington Post* in great detail or the *Star* in great detail or the *New York Times* in great detail or the *Baltimore Sun* in great detail, one could not possibly find out how the elections were run in Vietnam in 1967. One could find an incredible amount of analysis of the election of 1967 in Vietnam. One could find God knows how many things, but one could not find out how the elections were run. If one wanted to make an analysis of the analyses there was literally nothing that anyone of us could use to check. This is a very real problem from the point of view of researchers. Whom does it serve? It doesn't really serve us.

MR. GEYELIN: I feel they have discussed the actual mechanics.

PROFESSOR PENNIMAN: No.

MR. GEYELIN: Then I suspect the reason we didn't is that you were looking from your vantage point which is certainly rational. I suspect that a reporter from his vantage point knew full well that this was a contest which was not terribly rational, and that the mechanics were not as important as what was going on in the dark of night, and what was going on in a lot of other ways, like who was going to be a candidate and who wasn't, like who was going to go to jail for trying to be a candidate and a lot of other things that were much more important, for a country which never had an election before, than the mechanics. I don't think that's what people are interested in. I don't think people have to understand the electoral machinery to know what's going on. I would agree with that judgment.

MR. CATER: You have raised a point that Mr. Geyelin touched on in his paper which I found rather interesting and disconcerting. He says that we have become so obsessed with the aberrations of the norm that frequently the norm does not get communicated. I think that this is a basic problem of communications in our society. We do live in a society now where we are more vitally concerned with what's happening all over, in which we have a greater sense of inner tension than ever before. If the norm—what is happening to most—does not get communicated, then the aberrations become meaningless.

MR. GEYELIN: I think it's a baffling problem but you can't get people to read things they're not interested in. People generally aren't interested in reading about the 75 percent of college campuses that are quiet, but when the administration building at Harvard is sacked, this has something to do with what the market is.

PROFESSOR PENNIMAN: But why, when media talk about Vietnam, to go back to my case in point, would it not be reasonable to state that this is what the constitutional provisions are, and that this is an action of the national assembly and not of the Ky regime? This becomes quite crucial to the content of the decision. Furthermore, the question of how you run an election is related to the question whether or not 34.8 percent is a significant margin, over other candidates.

VOICE: It is to the political scientist, but I don't think it is to the average reader.

PROFESSOR PENNIMAN: This merely indicates that the media are free to make it impossible for anyone to analyze the election except as one outguesses the biases of those who wrote the pieces. If not outrageous, it is at least difficult for the average reader.

MR. GEYELIN: To go back to your original comment about writing the music, I have a different kind of an answer. The press does not write the score, but obviously every newspaper plays it differently. You can see that on any front page or in any two stories of the same event. But you can also see it in any two accounts of the same automobile accident. I'm not sure what that proves.

GARY BAYER, Office of Congressman Clarence J. Brown: I address this to both of them, but particularly to Mr. Geyelin who seems more on the offensive about the monopoly system. I was wondering if he would comment on, if not the Vice President's Iowa speeches, at least the thesis that there are dangers in having only three major television networks. I think Walter Cronkite's audience is about 25 million people every night and Huntley-Brinkley's is as large if not larger. The *Washington Post's* circulation is 500,000 or so and the *New York Times'* is a million or something like that, which is a drop in the bucket as compared to what Walter Cronkite or Huntley-Brinkley have. How does this fit into the problem of only three networks and three network news services?

MR. GEYELIN: I think part of it is something to which Mr. Cater alluded and with which I certainly agree. One of the reasons I think British television news is so good is that there is—I'm not sure we want it here—but there is a public television network. It plays against a private one and I suspect that they tend to keep each other honest. But reading the Vice President's case—I went back and read everything—he rested it very largely on that particular occasion of the commentary after the President's speech. I went back and read every bit of it, and I saw some of it that night and it was really thoroughly antiseptic. Now there might have been something terribly exciting about the eyebrows and so forth, but if you read the text you know they leaned very far over backwards. Then the moment he spoke, not the networks so much but the affiliates began shutting off these commentaries. I tell you there are correctives if people think it's loaded. There's one thing they can do which is absolutely devastating, which is turn it off. Network executives react to the noise of buttons turning off faster than anything and so do the affiliates.

MR. BAYER: I totally disagree with the Vice President's point about analysis. It seems to me that when the President of the United States is given free prime time, at the very least he ought to be willing to subject himself to critical comment, and as far as I know the President is willing.

MR. GEYELIN: You're talking about not enough outlets?

MR. BAYER: Yes, the very least he ought to be able to subject himself to when he has 50 million viewers prime time is someone else coming on and saying whether they disagree with him. I don't disagree with that. What I am talking about—and Cronkite made that point—is that the TV networks only cater to what's wrong with our society. I think Agnew mentioned that. Even leaving aside whether or not they have the right to analyze the President, how do you make sure that what the TV networks do on their 6:30 news is responsible enough—because of their fantastic influence on the public?

MR. GEYELIN: I don't know how you handle that. I don't think you can make sure they're giving an adequate picture. All I am saying is this. It's going to remain as a free commercial operation. It's going to be somewhat at the mercy of the ratings and the ratings I think unfortunately, have less to do with the quality of the picture that is presented of American society and somewhat more to do with how telegenic the newscaster is.

MR. BAYER: It seems to me that, from Agnew's speech on, the media reacted with—Oh, my gosh! A government official has criticized us. There had been some criticism of the media prior to Agnew, no question about that. But every media person I've ever seen has granted that they were not critical enough of themselves. There were excesses and they never criticized themselves. The Vice President came in and criticized you and the media said "Why, the Vice President criticized us; why, that shouldn't happen. I don't know who should criticize us but it ought not to be a government official." I'm not sure whom you think ought to criticize you, I guess you think you ought to do it yourselves but that wasn't being done either.

MR. CATER: Well, I disagree with that analysis. When the Vice President did it, of course, the three networks interrupted their nightly news programs to carry the full text of it. Other people have been doing it, to a degree, and that is not news. So here again, the networks were sort of hoisting themselves on their own petard of news judgment. I don't know where you would get on that particular line of argument.

MR. GEYELIN: There is no question—I don't think—that the press shouldn't be criticized. It started with Jefferson. Criticizing the press has been engaged in by every President who has led anything like an exciting life in office and I don't think anyone objects to public officials criticizing. I go back to what I said earlier, the nature of this criticism is really so inadequate and off the point that you had to wonder what the point really was. That's all I'm really saying.

DONALD R. LARRABEE, Griffin-Larrabee News Bureau: I gather, then, that you favor an investigative commission. I didn't hear Phil say anything about that, but I suspect that this isn't your solution. Ralph Nader has made quite a reputation shaking up certain professions and industries. I think he has been encouraged by the press a great deal, at least his investigations have been given a good play. I wonder if he might be the man to lead up an inquiry into the press. Do you have any comment on that?

MR. GEYELIN: I would be very thoroughly in favor of it. How could we not be in favor of it? He is a free agent. I don't know what the royal commission theory is exactly, but it's an independent, nongovernmental operation as far as I understand and I have absolutely no objection to that. In fact, I think the more the merrier.

MR. CATER: I think the Nader Raider analysis is one that hadn't occurred to me. The amount of corrective good that man has been able to do by skillful organizing of intelligence is, I think, very heartening.

STEPHEN J. McCORMICK, Mutual Broadcasting System: Incidentally Mr. Agnew's name has been kicked around quite a bit. I think the comment might well be made that of all the Vice Presidents any of us have known, for the time we've been around, no one has caused more comment about news and communications than we've had in this country in the last six months. But if he hadn't made those speeches who would ever have known of Agnew? I think this has been a good thing, that he should stimulate the discussions. Incidentally I didn't speak for any of the television networks but when Agnew made his blast I did put out a statement for the network I represent, 525 radio stations. I said we supported the thrust of his remarks, which sought responsibility and accuracy and balance and fairness, within the realm of possibility and objectivity. I think this is what he had in mind. I think the speech was pretty—well, it isn't the sort of thing any of us would have written.

I think he has missed the big point, that in terms of national and international news, most of the coverage is given to our audience all over the world from the wire services. He made no comment to speak of on the roles that the wire services play. If you take any day in the week, with over 5,000 radio stations in operation, a wire service story comes on the ticker and you know it's on the air just like that. Television may wait a few hours to put together a package. The newspaper has more time, the news machine has more time. It goes on radio, immediately, to an audience that's rarely thought of, some 70 million auto radios. Once it's there, it's there. When the retraction comes in or the correction or the analysis or the other approach that goes on the air too, but you've relevance to the earlier account. These are areas I think the Vice President might well have talked about.

I might add one other thought: American news organizations are private, profit-making organizations unlike those in other parts of the world. And we are competitive. And quite often being competitive, as you pointed out, we move so fast that we make mistakes. And in that regard, the third string film editor for a television show might have much more control than would a vice president, producer, or director or a team. I understand that over 300 people put together the Huntley-Brinkley show. It might well be that some fellow way down the line has made the decision of what film will be shown and won't be shown. In terms of effect on the news I disagree that all impact comes just with our reporting it. I think we oftentimes cause it to happen in the hours and days ahead. And in recent years I think we've proven that fact. Especially with the electronics side.

A. J. MONTGOMERY, Office of Senator Jack Miller: Wes Gallagher then an executive of the Associated Press made the comment—and I am paraphrasing—that the courts can protect freedom of the press and communications media but they cannot inspire public confidence in journalism. This can only come from journalism's own performance. Isn't the fundamental question, then, has journalism's own performance inspired public confidence? Isn't that the real issue which inspired the outpouring of public reaction to Agnew's comments in Des Moines, Montgomery, and others?

MR. CATER: Mr. Rap. Brown's picture of society is presumably somewhat different than George Wallace's and yet they would probably find mutual agreement in

the two major points of Agnew. One is that the picture
of America that is being communicated by the media
is not the picture he sees and two, that somebody up
there is tampering with it. There is a diverse band of
brothers that support this view. I don't think we get
very far looking at it from the devil view. I do think
that the media have done an amazing job of communication. But the time has come and the system has
developed to the point where we need to look at it
again. If AT&T still ran their switchboards the way
they used to, there would not be enough women in
America to handle the traffic. Well, the communication media don't have the opportunity to automate
reporting. But this is no reason for not investigating
how the job can be improved. We're in an era when
public confidence has been withdrawn from almost
everybody. It's not just the media that are suffering
this loss of confidence. Damn few preachers really have
the confidence of the communities anymore.

MR. GEYELIN: Basically I agree with that about
confidence and I do think the other thing, which is the
point I tried to make, is that in the first place people
don't want to believe that things are as bad as they
sound and in the second place, of course, they are not.
People who are living in the great quiet parts of the
country cannot find any evidence to sustain what they
see on their television screens and the front pages of
their newspapers. But that doesn't necessarily mean
that it's less significant on that account. It doesn't take

a great many people to disrupt a university. It doesn't take a great many people to throw fear into a whole town. It takes 40 crank phone calls and one bomb scare to put New York on its ear. That's not a large segment of the population that's in revolt against the Establishment, but it is quite large enough to be a serious factor. So therefore, the reaction may be hysterical, in a sense, may be overdrawn. But I'd much rather have it that way, than the other way because the problem has to be there. We have got this problem even though you might not see it. The reader of a weekly newspaper in a small town that hasn't really been touched by it yet—and that's the vast majority of the country—I think that they may not see it and may wonder who's conning whom, but it doesn't mean that it isn't there.

MR. MONTGOMERY: You think that public confidence exists, then?

MR. GEYELIN: It depends on where and to what degree. I think that what Mr. Cater says is right. All establishments are undergoing a crisis of confidence. That includes the Supreme Court, the United States Senate, the press, the Church, the universities, anywhere there is authority, responsibility or power lies. People are taking second looks.

KENNETH SPARKS, U.S. Information Agency: Mr. Geyelin, there are some of us, at least two in this room and maybe more who worked for awhile with a government agency that Mr. Cater referred to, the Office of Economic Opportunity. We probably shouldn't speak of it in the past tense. But it was an agency (that still exists) that did a lot of things right and it did a lot of things wrong. I think if you were to weigh the amount of material that was published about the agency you would come out with a scale tipped very heavily towards favorable stories. The problem was that most of those stories were feature stories that appeared on the back pages.

I wonder if one thing we couldn't do in the journalism profession to improve the coverage of government would be to correct this one thing that we saw time after time at OEO: The story of the sensational nature getting all the play, and frequently the wrong story. Time and time again, sensational stories, particularly I think, by the wire services and oftentimes by the regional wire services, also by some of the columnists, would get a great deal of attention. Then the opposite side of the story would be covered the following day, if at all, on the back page, where the comment was good. I wonder if some little corrective might be worked out within the profession, say getting the editors, publishers, and maybe the guild and some others together, which would probably be no small trick. Could we organize some sort of a group, representing at least those three interests, to which people could send complaints and have some follow-up action taken on the thing? I don't think that many people argue against the standard of at least checking another source, and maybe including in the story that such and such a source was checked.

It can be stated that these other sources had no answer or they had an answer and we think it's baloney or whatever. But at least we could make sure that those sources were checked so it's not this terrible game between the press and the bureaucracy, the bureaucracy trying sometimes to catch up to reports that were one-sided.

MR. GEYELIN: Well, you're really talking about what should be a guiding standard for all good reporters and certainly when charges are made against, say the President of the United States, the White House is usually checked. Mr. Ziegler either has a comment or has no comment. That kind of thing is done. I'm sure there are areas where it isn't done or isn't done enough. I don't think it's a chronic weakness but I think it's bad journalism that you're describing and honestly it ought to be better. Whether you could get a kind of code of some kind of standards, I don't know. But I think that during this period of public criticism of the media some newspapers are thinking in terms of new approaches of just this kind.

The *Louisville Courier-Journal* has done something that is quite interesting, which is to establish an in-house ombudsman. This is not just a kind of natural process but a man to speak for the public, so to speak, to stand outside of the chain of command of the newspaper, with responsibility to the publisher and nobody else, to read the paper every day, to listen to the complaints, and to bring them to the responsible editors and reporters as kind of a conscience built into the newspaper. I think this is an interesting idea. It may be that more papers ought to do it. But I don't know if there is any quick fix for human frailties of this kind.

STEPHEN BANKER, Canadian Broadcasting Corporation: I have some scattershot comments that I would appreciate having your reaction to. First of all, I think you're dead wrong when you talk about the great silent parts of our country where people don't see what all the fuss is about. There are no such places left. Last year I did a story—a series of stories—about the town of Riceville, Iowa, population 1,000. I found out that the kids there—most of whom had never seen a black person—had highly structured prejudices about black people that fit into the patterns of Los Angeles, New York, or Washington or whatever. In other words, they had lived through the black revolt, it had come home to them in several ways, some sick ways that the rest of the country had experienced.

Secondly, one gentleman talked about the press concentrating on the bad or the unfortunate elements of society, and I ask you, Sir, whether you think that's true; whether it should be that way; or whether in fact the press shouldn't even make a judgment on what an aspect of society is, whether it is bad or good? And lastly, I was interested to hear that your reaction to Mr. Mollenhoff was—in talking about subpoenas—entirely on a pragmatic level: "It dries up our sources!" Is there a moral question there?

MR. GEYELIN: Well, I didn't mean to put it entirely on a pragmatic basis. It does interfere with the proper functioning, in my opinion, of the press. It is very hindering; you can't work well under those conditions. I think you have to have the right of confidentiality in order to function.

Where it becomes a moral question is where you are obliged to violate it (a confidence) or go to jail.

MR. BANKER: So you see nothing wrong with the press working arm-in-arm with the government as long as it's completely secret and the sources don't know about it?

MR. GEYELIN: No, I see everything wrong with it. I see a lot that's right with the press working arm-in-arm with the government if the source does know about it. A reporter can tell the source before he starts "If you tell me anything incriminating, if you tell me you're going to commit a crime, I'm going to tell the police." Normally it depends on the kind of journalism you practice and working in Washington you don't normally talk to people who tell you they're going to commit a crime. But out around the country where it is a crime to cross state lines to engage in a conspiracy you can talk to kids who will tell you they're going to commit a crime and in fact are going to commit a crime because they want to go to jail. So that I think that raises a different kind of question.

At the greatest extreme, you would turn in every piece of film you have of the events in Dallas in

November 1963 without hesitation. If somebody told you they planned to assassinate a public official, or burn down the *Washington Post* or tear up Dow Chemical across the street, I think you probably would tell the police. But it really depends on the circumstances in which this confidence is given to you and whether you think the overriding necessity is to save lives. To answer your question about the responsibility if you report bad news—I've sort of forgotten what——

MR. BANKER: Well, he just said the press is concentrating on the bad or unfortunate elements in society.

MR. GEYELIN: Well, I went into that and I think Mr. Cater did too. It does concentrate on the bad because people are, by nature, more interested in the bad than in the good. I did mention, I think, that there is a process where after you focused on the aberrations long enough the norm becomes interesting. The news media ought to look around from time to time and find out whether there isn't a hell of a good story about campus X where there isn't student protest.

You may be right in that there is no part of the country that hasn't been touched by this or at least where the kids are not touched by it. But I think there are parts where they are not touched by it anything like the way they are in other parts—not just the kids but older people do not see the ferment around them that they see on television. I don't know how much of the country that is but I think probably there are some people like that.

JOHANN BENSON, Legislative Reference Service: When you said that the norm becomes interesting, I'm not so sure that it is that interesting that it would last for any length of time. That is, you might report one incident of the quieting down of campuses. Do you really think that you would report many of them such as you would report a violent action on the campus?

Let me ask one other question, if I may, which was primary in my mind. That was with respect to Vice President Agnew. Do you think that he has made any permanent impression on the way news is reported?

I ask this because I saw an interview with Walter Cronkite—he was on the Martin Agronsky show—and he confessed, I would say, that he was intimidated but he was careful to add afterwards that (it was) not him personally but he was sure that the industry had been intimidated. I wonder if you feel that there are some prevailing intimidations whether salubrious or pernicious.

MR. GEYELIN: I think there are and even if there aren't we're being accused of it. You get it coming and going in this situation. Already the Democrats are saying that the press has stopped asking hard questions about Laos, which strikes me as a little bit silly; or has stopped asking hard questions about Judge Carswell which also strikes me as a little silly. But in any case that accusation is now being made.

I am told that the networks—some network executives, at any rate, are not so much intimidated themselves as anxious about the degree of intimidation of the affiliates. In their communities the network affiliates are worried about Agnew and feeling the heat a lot more directly and therefore they are not much interested in running commentary after presidential speeches. I think it's worth noting. Maybe it's sheer accident and maybe the networks can explain it, but when Mobilization, which was really quite a spectacle and lasted all day, was not covered live by television. It may be that it didn't lend itself to live coverage. It wasn't even covered, as I recall, by a kind of one hour special that evening, from film clips taken that day. It was covered in the regular news shows. It, of course, followed the Des Moines speech. I wouldn't allege and I haven't got the slightest evidence that there was any kind of cause and effect there. The point has been made, but I don't know.

VOICE: I don't think there's any more intimidation—I think that word is ridiculous. Networks aren't licensed by the commission, therefore they're not worried. But some of them do own stations. Stations are concerned. There is far more examination, with a fine tooth comb, of every license renewal application before the commission now than there ever was before the Agnew speech. And this will continue, obviously.

MR. GEYELIN: Well, the remark was made by Herb Klein in public as well as in private that the Agnew speech is the greatest guarantee that those currently applying for television licenses would get them. I think you're probably right.

MR. CATER: I wish to address myself to the point about "the norm becomes interesting." We have reached the point where we wonder in the public and in the government, too, whether anything works. Stories that speak out and try to find where a community has done something that works are good journalism. I do think it can be made interesting and that there is a public for these stories. Otherwise, we are in pretty bad shape.

MR. GEYELIN: I think this is happening. We had a story today about how the British have conquered or are beginning to conquer the air pollution in London and pollution of the Thames. I think that's extremely readable. Actually enough people, as I say, have had enough and would like to have some ray of hope.

VERA GLASER, Knight Newspapers: This is addressed to Mr. Geyelin. You made a very flat statement in your initial presentation that there is no threat in common ownership of newspapers and television stations. It is quite possible that you documented that in your paper in some section that I didn't read but, I would like to have, perhaps, a little rationale for that. Does that indicate that you are not concerned at all about the trend toward amalgamation in the communications media?

MR. GEYELIN: No, I don't think that there is no threat. I think that at the moment, there is no real monopoly of news outlets. But very obviously, there are fewer newspapers than there used to be and there are more one newspaper towns. I would like to stand corrected on Montgomery, Alabama. It was my dumb luck to pick Mr. Cater's home town. (Laughter.) It's a one-newspaper town, not a one-voice town. And there are a lot more of them. According to Professor Nixon of Minnesota there are just a lot fewer one-voice towns. And as I cited in the quotation from him he sees in this a sort of a built-in continuing corrective that keeps everybody a little more honest. I also pointed out that the most powerful, most significant elements in all this are the wire services, and they are generally overlooked. I don't know what would happen in this country if one of them—we have already lost one—if we lost another. I think then we would have a very serious problem of a lack of competition, of a monopoly situation. They are all pervasive.